Dating

"What Is a Healthy Relationship?"

by Kate Havelin

Consultant:
Martha Farrell Erickson, PhD
Director of Children, Youth, and Family Consortium
University of Minnesota

Perspectives on Relationships

LifeMatters
an imprint of Capstone Press
Mankato, Minnesota

LifeMatters books are published by Capstone Press
818 North Willow Street • Mankato, Minnesota 56001
http://www.capstone-press.com

Printed in the United States of America

Library of Congress Cataloging-in-Publication Data
Havelin, Kate, 1961–
     Dating: what is a healthy relationship? / by Kate Havelin
         p.   cm.—(Perspectives on relationships)
     Includes bibliographical references and index.
     ISBN 0-7368-0292-4 (book).—ISBN 0-7368-0295-9 (series)
     1. Dating (Social customs)—Juvenile literature. 2. Interpersonal
relations in adolescence—Juvenile literature. 3. Teenagers—Sexual
behavior—Juvenile literature. 4. Sexual ethics for teenagers—Juvenile literature.
     I. Title. II. Series.
     HQ801.H368   2000
     306.73—dc21   99-32713
                                     CIP

YA
306.73

Staff Credits

Rebecca Aldridge, Kristin Thoennes, editors; Adam Lazar, designer; Kimberly Danger, photo researcher

Photo Credits
Cover: ©PhotoDisc/Barbara Penoyar
Index Stock Imagery/6
Index Stock Photography/14, 38, 59
©PhotoDisc/Barbara Penoyar, 37
Photri, Inc/11; ©Bachmann, 15, 31, 58; ©Dennis MacDonald, 42; ©Brent Jones, 45
PNI/©DigitalVision 46; ©RubberBall, 28
Unicorn Stock Photos/©Robert Ginn, 27; ©Steve Bourgeois, 34; ©Eric R. Berndt, 51; ©Jeff Greenberg, 52; ©Karen Holsinger Mullen, 55
UP Magazine/©Tim Yoon, 8
Visuals Unlimited/©Jeff Greenberg, 23

A 0 9 8 7 6 5 4 3 2 1

Table of Contents

This book provided by a
grant from the
Family Resource Council
Merced County
Office of Education

Chapter Overview

Dating means that two people who are attracted to each other and find each other special spend time together.

It is natural for teens to be curious about dating and sexuality. Hormones, or natural chemicals in the body, make teens more sexually aware.

Dating does not guarantee happiness.

Chapter 1

What Is Dating All About?

It's the first day of high school. Patsy, Jonah, and Will are nervous and excited.

First Day Back

The kids around them all seem older. Even the kids they knew before seem to have changed during the summer. Some are taller. Some look older. Everyone seems cool, but the change is kind of overwhelming.

Patsy overhears two girls she knew in eighth grade talking about their boyfriends. Will hears that two classmates, Michelle and Abdul, have been going out all summer. Even Jonah is talking about girls in whom he is interested. Patsy and Will feel awkward. They do not feel ready to date. Somehow everyone else around them seems to know more about dating.

Dating is spending time with a special person whom you care about. It is like every other part of life. Some people start earlier, and some start later. Some people seem more comfortable than others with dating. Almost everyone dates at some time.

Why People Date

People date for many reasons.

Dating teaches you about other people and yourself.
Spending time with one person is a good way to get to know that person. It also helps you learn about other types of people. You learn about yourself by seeing how your reactions to dating differ from those of your friends.

Dating can be fun.
Finding a girlfriend or boyfriend can make a person feel more special. It is exciting and fun to like and be liked. Romance can make a person feel happy, content, beautiful, funny, or smart.

Everyone else is dating.

Teens often pay attention to what their peers do. When one group of teens tries something new, other teens may become more curious. Dating is something many but not all young people want to try. Popular media such as movies, television, and music also push the idea that everyone is dating. However, the fact is that many teens do not date.

It's a natural instinct.

Hormones affect some of the attraction we feel toward people. These natural chemicals control body functions and help young bodies grow. During puberty, a teen's body starts to change. Sex organs mature. For example, a girl's breasts develop and grow. At the same time, girls experience an increase in levels of the hormones estrogen and progesterone. The hormone testosterone increases in boys.

Hormones cause people to think more about sex. They stimulate a person's sexual desire. This is natural. They may cause teens to want a close, special relationship.

Waiting to Date

People mature at different times and in different ways. Some teens may not want to date. That is normal. Friends may try to push some teens to date before they are ready. Teens should listen to themselves. There is no deadline for when a person must begin dating. Teens should date only when they feel ready.

Eleanor loves science class. She thinks her

Eleanor Admires Her Teacher

teacher, Ms. Flanders, is funny and smart. Eleanor wishes she could be like Ms. Flanders. Eleanor hangs around after school to see Ms. Flanders before she leaves.

Sometimes Eleanor wonders if she is normal. She does not tell her friends how much she thinks about Ms. Flanders. She believes they would laugh at her and think she was weird. Eleanor just cannot stop thinking about Ms. Flanders.

Attraction to the Same Sex

Many teens have a crush on someone of the same gender, or sex. That means a boy may have a crush on another male, or a girl may have a crush on another female. This does not mean their attractions are homosexual. You can have a same-sex crush and still have heterosexual, or opposite-sex, attractions. It is common for teens to experience attraction to both genders.

Learning to be comfortable with your own attractions is important. The essential thing is to be who you are. Once you accept who you are, you are more likely to find others who will accept you.

Family battles over suitable dates for young people are nothing new. William Shakespeare's play, *Romeo and Juliet,* is about two feuding families who do not want their kids to fall in love.

This book is for all teens who are curious about dating. However, it does not focus on specific homosexual issues. Teens who are concerned about having same-sex attractions may benefit from talking with someone supportive.

When Parents Disapprove

Some parents think their teens are too young to date. Not everyone agrees at which age dating is okay. Parents may have trouble accepting that their teens are ready to date. Those parents may try to control a teen's normal urge to be independent.

It can be hard to have parents who do not want you to date. Some teens disobey their parents. They date secretly. That can cause tension and lessen the joy of dating. Other teens try to prove to their parents that they are mature enough to date. They might show this by following the curfew their parents set. Such an action can help parents see that their teens are responsible.

Not all societies allow or encourage dating. The numbers of young Americans who date often surprises teens who move to the United States from other countries. For example, high school students from Taiwan, Malaysia, and Colombia showed such surprise. They all said dating was less common in their country than in the United States.

Some parents disapprove of the specific person their son or daughter wants to date. Parents may think someone is too old, too sexy, too rich, or too poor. Some parents do not want their teens to date anyone from a different religion or race. Mixed-race dating may be an issue for some parents. No laws prohibit interracial relationships. However, many mixed-race couples experience prejudice.

Teens should talk with parents who disapprove of the person they are seeing. Teens may find parents have some good reasons for their concern. Sometimes love makes it hard for a person to see the faults in someone he or she is dating.

Dating Does Not Equal Happiness

Our society sends countless messages that romance solves everything. Think about Cinderella. Life, however, is not a fairy tale or a movie. Even people who truly love one another do not marry and just live happily ever after. Dating, love, and marriage do not guarantee happiness.

Respecting and caring about yourself can improve your chances for happiness. People who love themselves are more likely to find others who also will love them. It helps to learn to listen to yourself. Once you know yourself, it's easier to figure out what kind of person you want to date.

Points to Consider

How would you explain dating to someone from Mars?

Why do you think parents are concerned about whom their teens date?

Do you think parents treat boys and girls equally when it comes to dating? Explain.

How would your family react if you dated someone of a different race or religion?

Chapter Overview

Almost everyone needs time to get comfortable with learning how to date.

Before you begin dating, it helps to think about what you are doing to make a good first impression.

It's important to think about why you are attracted to a person and what you know about him or her.

You can get to know a person you like by talking with him or her.

Chapter 2

Tips for Starting to Date

Miles Feels Left Behind

Andrew and Miles have been friends since fourth grade. But now Miles worries that he cannot keep up with Andrew. Andrew is popular with girls. Miles does not have a girlfriend. Sometimes Andrew arranges a double date for his friend. But usually Miles is left behind.

Miles does not understand how dating comes so easily for Andrew. Andrew talks casually to girls. He can flirt. Miles gets tongue-tied. He feels shy and embarrassed around girls. Andrew tells him it is easy to talk with girls. Miles disagrees.

There is no formula for dating success. However, there are many ways to improve your chances for success and fun. You can learn about relationships by watching other people. Maybe you have a friend who seems popular. What does he or she do to make friends? Chances are that your friend talks with new people. The tips in this chapter may help you get to know people.

Look at Yourself

Teens who want to date or just make new friends should try to make a good first impression. You probably form an opinion of someone the first time you meet that person. Likewise, the first time a new person sees you often shapes his or her opinion of you.

To make a positive impression, check yourself out in the mirror. Is your hair clean? Have you brushed your teeth? Have you bathed? Those basic grooming habits do make a difference. When you are well groomed, you feel good about yourself and that shows.

Next, think of how you look when you walk down the hall at school. Do you smile and say hi to people? Or do you slouch and stare at the ground to avoid looking at people? Many teens feel unhappy with their looks. You may not feel comfortable with every part of your body right now. However, you can work on feeling comfortable with yourself. For example, you might try smiling, even if you hate your braces.

Some teens try too hard to make a good first impression. Every head in the room does not have to turn when you enter. You do not have to say or wear outrageous things. The most important thing is to feel comfortable with yourself.

Look at the Person You Are Attracted To

You may know someone you think you would like to date. How do you know if the two of you should date? To answer that question, spend some time finding out about the person. Is he or she nice to friends? How does he or she treat other people? You may no longer be interested once you find out how that person treats others.

Think about why you are attracted to a certain person. Are you interested mainly because of how he or she looks? Relationships that are based on appearances are usually shallow. Healthy relationships need to be based on more than looks.

It helps to listen to what other friends think of the person you are interested in. However, it's important not to be completely swayed by hearsay. Try to get a feeling for yourself about what someone is like. Then think about why you are attracted to that person.

Talking does not have to be face-to-face. You may feel more comfortable talking on the phone with a new friend. You may even communicate via e-mail. Find out if the person you like has an e-mail address. Then send him or her a short note.

Talk With the Person You Like

The best way to get to know someone is to talk with that person. Talking will help you discover what the two of you have in common. Does the person you admire seem only to care about football? If you do not care about sports, you may decide that person is not for you. What kind of music does he or she like? You may find that you both like the same bands. Going to a concert together could be a natural idea for a first date.

Often teens get crushes on others but are too shy to approach them. Sometimes it takes courage to talk with a person you like. If you like someone, you might try these strategies.

Strike up a conversation with the person.

Practice things to say before approaching the person.

Try out lines at home. Rehearse alone in front of the mirror or with a friend. The more you practice, the more comfortable you will become talking with potential dates.

Make eye contact. It helps to look a person in the eye during conversation.

Some people think the hardest part of a conversation is getting started. You might start by asking people how they are doing. For example, ask a classmate how he did on the history quiz. Ask the person whose locker is near yours what she did last weekend.

Serena's First Big Step

Serena is shy. She feels too embarrassed to talk with boys. Serena has a crush on the new boy in math class, José. Serena's friend Amy persuades Serena to show her feelings.

Serena takes a big step. She finds out where José's locker is. One day she stops to tie her shoe near José while he is opening his locker. José says hi. Serena asks him if he likes this new school. José says it's okay, but he has not met many kids yet.

Serena and José walk toward their last class of the day. Serena asks José about his old school. He is happy to talk about something he knows well. He asks Serena if she wants to study for the math test after school.

They agree to meet at the library. Serena feels excited and a little scared. This is better than a daydream. Serena has never been so eager to study math.

Points to Consider

Do you know how your parents met? What memories do your parents have of dating?

Why do you think first impressions are so important?

What influences your first impression of a new person?

How often do you talk with new people? Is it easier to meet new people alone or with friends? Explain.

Chapter Overview

It is not always easy to see the difference between love and a crush. In general, love lasts while crushes quickly fade.

Crushes are normal. Even crushes on famous people can be a safe and healthy way to learn about relationships.

Love and sex are not the same thing. Sexual intercourse doesn't prove love for a person.

Spending money isn't necessary to prove you care about someone. Just being together and having fun can be enough.

Chapter 3

Is It a Crush, or Is It Love?

Three Friends, Three Kinds of Love

Maya, Ingrid, and Lisa are best friends. Maya loves a rock star. Ingrid says she loves Robert. Ingrid feels nervous when Robert is around, so she rarely talks with him. Lisa is sure she is in love with Todd. They have been dating for four months.

Lisa believes her friends just have crushes. However, she does not say that to them. She knows it would hurt their feelings.

Lisa dreams about marrying Todd. She gets angry when her mother calls Lisa's feelings for Todd a crush. Lisa is certain her love will last forever. However, even she wonders how to tell real love from a crush.

Love is a powerful feeling. One day love can make you feel wonderful. The next day it can disappoint you and make you feel miserable. How do you know if you are in love? How can you tell the difference between infatuation, or a crush, and love?

It's hard to distinguish between a crush and love. Usually the difference between the two becomes clear over time. In the beginning, you may feel strong emotions for someone. If those feelings fade within a few weeks, however, they probably were not feelings of love. The following chart contrasts a crush and love.

Crush or love?

Crush	Love
Can happen immediately	Usually takes time to develop
Can involve a stranger or someone you barely know	Involves a person whose strengths and weaknesses you know
Can involve the same feelings toward a different person every month	Usually does not happen frequently
Feels like your heart is in more control than your head	Feels like your heart and head are both in control
Involves someone you think is perfect	Involves someone who you know isn't perfect but care for anyway
Can end as suddenly as it started	Usually takes time to end

CityKids, a New York City group that promotes young people's respect, asked kids what they thought when they heard the word *love.* Some of the responses included:

- "Makes you cry"
- "Unconditional feeling"
- "Feels good!"
- "Never had it"
- "Happy"
- "Beautiful"

You Do Not Have to Figure Out Whether It's Love

The line between like and love may not be clear. Sometimes that does not matter. You can like a person a great deal without knowing for certain if you are in love. Two people can be happy together and have a deep crush on one another. A person does not have to be truly in love to care for someone.

Crushes Can Be a Safe Way to Learn About Love

Crushes from afar can sometimes be helpful. Many teens admire musicians, actors, or athletes. Chances are, you will never meet the star you dream about. However, you may learn to adjust to the strong feelings you have. You may become comfortable with the feeling of being attracted to someone. Then you can set your sights on someone you really can meet or may already know.

It also is normal to have a crush on someone close to you. For example, you may have a crush on someone in your class. It can be fun to imagine what a relationship would be like with that person. You may choose to keep your crush a romantic dream. Maybe you want to try to get to know him or her. Sometimes getting to know the person destroys the dream. Other times getting to know someone is more fun than a dream.

Myth: Sexual intercourse is the best way to show you love someone.

Fact: Sex is not the same as love. Sexual intercourse does not prove you love someone.

Love and Sex Are Not the Same

It is important to keep in mind that love is not the same thing as having sex. Love and sex can be completely separate. You can love someone and never have sex with that person. Some people have sex with people they do not love. Sexual intercourse, or penetration of the penis into the vagina or anus, can be part of a loving relationship. However, it is not a necessary ingredient for love.

Some people confuse love and sex. They may pressure others to have sex to prove their love. However, having sex does not prove love for someone. People who pressure their partner to have intercourse show disrespect for the partner. It is never okay to pressure a person to have sex.

Money Cannot Buy Love

It is possible to love someone without spending a lot of money. For example, you do not need to buy jewelry, flowers, or other gifts to prove you care. The best way to show you care is to be kind, gentle, considerate, and thoughtful. You could try asking about your boyfriend or girlfriend's day and listening to the answer. Spending money does not prove you love someone. Two people who care about each other can have fun just talking or engaging in free activites.

Points to Consider

How do you define love? How do you define a crush?

Why do you think people have crushes on professional athletes or musicians whom they will never meet?

Have you had a crush on someone? If so, did you get to know the person? What was getting to know the person like?

Why do you think so many people confuse love and sex?

Chapter Overview

Romance requires some privacy. It is best not to tell friends all about your dates.

Communication is important to make sure a relationship feels comfortable to both people.

It is important not to try to change who you are to please your date.

Going to isolated places when starting to date someone new can be dangerous. It is safer to stick to public places.

When you have a boyfriend or girlfriend, it is still important to take time out for yourself and other friends.

Chapter 4

Tips for Successful Dating

It takes practice to learn how to have successful relationships. Everyone makes some mistakes while dating. Sometimes teens have trouble understanding how to build strong ties with others. This chapter suggests some things you can do to improve your relationships.

Talk Less About Your Date

Many people want to let the world know how happy they are when they are in love. That's normal. It is not a good idea, however, to tell friends every detail about a date. Dating is a special relationship between two people. Part of what makes romance special is that it is only between the two people.

Did You Know?

Some of the keys to successful relationships are being loyal, trustworthy, honest, and respectful. Every healthy relationship involves some compromise. Both partners have to be willing to give and take.

People who tell all about their dates sometimes get burned. Friends may distort, or alter, things you tell them. You may end up getting a reputation you do not want or deserve. Your date may think you cannot keep a secret.

Take Your Time

You may want to become closer to the person you are dating. You may want to spend all your time with that special person. You may want to have sex with that person. However, two people rarely share the same feelings about how fast a relationship should grow. It is important for a couple to talk and decide together how the relationship should develop.

Often couples break up because one person pushes the other to do something. One person may want a lot of physical intimacy, or closeness. Another person may want a lot of emotional intimacy. The difference between what two people want can create tension in a relationship. That can lead to resentment, anger, and breakups. It helps to talk honestly about what you want and to listen to what your partner wants.

Trouble for Charlotte and Abe

Charlotte and Abe have been dating for three months. They really like each other, but lately the two have been fighting. Charlotte gets jealous when Abe spends time with other friends. She thinks love means being together constantly. Abe feels smothered. He thinks Charlotte wants to be too serious.

Charlotte also feels pushed. Abe wants to have sex. Charlotte does not feel ready. She wants to be close to Abe but not in that way. Abe cannot understand how Charlotte can love him but not want sex. The two pressure each other. They do not realize that by pushing each other, they are destroying their relationship.

Be Yourself

Our ideas about love and romance often are based on what we see other people do. Movies, television shows, music, and books can all influence people's notions of love. People try to change themselves to match images that the media creates. These images often are not realistic.

You may think you can make your boyfriend or girlfriend happy if you change. You may think that losing weight or acting tough, innocent, or worldly will improve your relationship. It is a mistake to try to change who you are to please someone else. You will end up feeling uncomfortable. After all, the person was attracted to you for who you are. If you become someone you're not, you may lose the relationship. If you cannot be yourself with someone, then you probably should not be with that person.

Jamie doesn't understand why her **Michael Tries Too Hard** boyfriend, Michael, has been acting differently lately. Michael thinks Jamie expects him to act tough like the guys in the movies.

Last night at the self-serve pizza place, Jamie and Michael ran into Michael's friends. They all shared a booth. Michael told Jamie to get plates and napkins for everyone. Jamie wondered why Michael was bossing her around. She got the items but was angry. Later, Michael told her to pour water for everyone. Jamie said no, and Michael got mad. Michael's friends felt awkward.

Later when they were alone, Jamie and Michael fought. They did not understand each other's behavior. Jamie started to cry. "I don't want you to boss me around," she told Michael. "I just want you to be my friend. Why can't you be the way you used to be?" Michael felt mixed up. He did not want to upset Jamie, but he did not know how to act naturally with her.

Avoid Tricky Situations

Dating is usually fun. However, it also can be dangerous or scary. The best way to have a good time is to avoid dangerous situations. When a relationship is starting, it is a good idea to do activities as a group. Many people double date or group date. That way, they are not alone with a person whom they are just getting to know.

It also is smart to do things in public places like restaurants, movie theaters, parks, or skating rinks. It is a mistake to go to lonely, or isolated, areas on a date. That could put you in danger. Your date could force you to do something you do not want to do. Too often, girls are forced to have sex with their dates. This is called date rape. It is a serious problem that happens to teens and adults.

It also is a good idea not to drink alcohol or use other drugs during a date. The influence of alcohol and other drugs can make it hard to think clearly. You may end up doing something embarrassing or dangerous. You may throw up. You may say things you do not mean. You may end up having unprotected sex. Alcohol and other drugs can blur thinking and change behavior. It is best not to do things that make you lose control.

Take Time for Yourself and for Other Friends

It is natural to want to spend lots of time with a boyfriend or girlfriend. However, it's important to maintain other relationships you already have. Your other friends matter. You are who you are partly because of friends.

It's important to make time for yourself, too. Everyone needs some time alone. You need time to do the things you like such as reading mysteries or listening to your favorite music. If you can learn to enjoy being alone, it can help you all of your life.

Points to Consider

Why do you think blabbing about a date to friends may end up hurting you?

Why do you think males and females sometimes want different kinds of relationships?

Have you ever had a friend who changed once he or she started dating? What did you think about that?

Why do you think it is important to learn to be happy being alone?

Chapter Overview

It's important to think about the responsibilities involved with sex before becoming sexually active.

Many teens choose to be abstinent and not to have sex.

You have the right to choose what you will and will not do with your body.

Chapter 5

Deciding About Sex

Sexual intercourse is a natural thing for dating partners to think about. Wanting sexual intercourse, not wanting it, and being confused or scared about it are all normal. Choosing to have sexual intercourse is a big decision. There are many questions to ask yourself. Parts of the decision depend on communication with your dating partner and knowing the responsibilities involved.

Some Questions to Ask Yourself

People often have intercourse without making a conscious decision about it. Some teens have sex because they feel pressure from their date or their friends. In fact, a large U.S. study on sex found that teens face enormous pressure about sex. However, it is important to make a decision that is right for you.

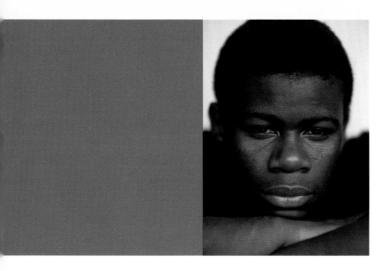

You might start by asking yourself questions like these.

Do I want to have sex yet?

Do I want to have sex with the person I am dating?

Why do I want to have sex?

Do I think having sex will change me, my partner, or our relationship?

What will happen to our relationship if I choose not to have sex?

Do I know how to prevent a possible pregnancy or a disease? Do I have what I need to prevent these?

Talk With Your Partner

Talking openly with your boyfriend or girlfriend is an important part of deciding whether to have sex. It's best to talk honestly about sex before it happens. One thing you need to discuss is how to prevent pregnancy and sexually transmitted diseases (STDs). Partners who cannot talk about birth control and protection should not have intercourse. Chapter 6 describes more about pregnancy and STDs.

Outercourse is a pleasurable alternative to sexual intercourse. It may include kissing, hugging, holding hands, or touching. Mutual masturbation is another kind of outercourse. It means that both partners enjoy rubbing or touching the sex organs. Outercourse also may include petting above or below the waist, body rubbing, or protected oral sex. Protection involves the use of a condom or dental dam to prevent STDs. It is best if couples talk in advance about what their limits will be during outercourse. It also is a good idea for couples to be prepared with protection in case they change their mind.

It's also important for each partner to talk about his or her sexual history. That way partners can know about the possibility of getting an STD from one another. Dating a person with an unknown sexual history can be risky.

The Responsibilities of Sex

Because sexual intercourse can result in pregnancy or an STD, it is important to have a plan. That means learning about options for preventing pregnancy. You and your partner may talk about the best method for the two of you. A health care provider can tell you about options for pregnancy prevention.

Being responsible about sex also means using protection to prevent an STD. Condoms prevent some STDs. Both male and female condoms can be purchased in drugstores and other stores. A dental dam is a kind of protection used during oral sex. A health care provider also can discuss protection with you.

You can change your mind about sex. Just because you have had sex once does not mean you must continue having sex. Abstinence is still a choice. You can postpone sex until a time in your life when you feel you are really ready.

Sex Can Lead to a Breakup

Some people think that sex strengthens the bond between partners. This may happen if the partners take time to build a strong relationship before having sex. However, sex often does not strengthen a relationship. Some people don't want a strong bond. Others become possessive, jealous, or overly sensitive once they have sex with a person. Such feelings often lead to the breakup of a relationship. It's best to take the time to build a relationship first. Then if you choose to have sex, it may be a meaningful expression of your feelings for one another.

Waiting Can Be Worth It

Many teens are not ready to have sex. They choose abstinence, or not to have sex for now. However, teens can choose abstinence and still date. It's possible to be physically close to someone without having sex.

Some teens feel less pressure when they choose abstinence. You may decide not to have intercourse but still try other kinds of romantic or sexual touch. You may decide you do not want any touching. Abstinence is a choice for now. You may simply choose to have intercourse at a later time in your life.

Brenda and James have been dating for several weeks. James has been pressuring Brenda to have sex. Brenda really likes James, but she just isn't ready for sex. One night, James pressures Brenda even more than usual.

Brenda Needs to Say No

"Come on, Brenda. Let's do it. Come on, you want it. I know you do. I love you. If you love me enough, you'll do it. Okay? Don't be scared."

Brenda stumbles over her words. "James, I uh . . . James, I love you. But, but . . . oh, don't do this to me. I'm not ready. Stop. I need you to stop."

What to Say When You're Not Ready for Sex

It is okay to say no to sex. It's your body, and you have the right to say no. However, saying no can be hard at times, especially if you really like the person. Sometimes a little practice can help you say no. You could try standing in front of a mirror when no one else can hear. Then you can practice saying the lines in the chart on the next page until you're comfortable.

Some Things to Say When You're Not Ready for Sex

"I'm not ready for sex yet."

"I don't want to get pregnant."

"Would you really have sex with someone who doesn't want it?"

"What's going to happen if we don't have sex?"

"Do you really want to be a parent yet?"

"I love you, and I don't want to mess things up between us."

"You're coming on too strong. I don't want to be with you right now."

"I have my period."

"No."

Points to Consider

Do you think there is a right age for everyone to have sex? Explain.

Why do you think it's best to discuss sex with a partner before it happens?

How do you think having sex soon after you start dating someone might harm your relationship?

Chapter Overview

Sexual intercourse can change your life forever.

Sexual intercourse can lead to pregnancy. Pregnancy forces teens to make some tough decisions about their life.

Sex can lead to STDs such as AIDS, herpes, or gonorrhea.

Chapter 6

What You Need to Know About Sex

Jessie gave birth to Kadeisha six weeks ago. She and the baby are living in her bedroom. Kadeisha's father doesn't help much. Jessie's parents help some.

Jessie Becomes a Mother

Kadeisha does not sleep through the night. Jessie has to get up and feed her. Jessie is tired and scared. She does not know how she will care for Kadeisha and handle school, which starts in a month. Jessie will have to come right home after school and take care of the baby.

"WAAAHHHH!!!!" Kadeisha is crying again. Jessie feels like crying, too. She wants to see her friends. She wants to sleep. She wants to have fun. Jessie realizes she will never be a teen just like her friends again. At 16, Jessie is a parent.

Sexual intercourse can be a pleasurable experience. However, it involves some risks as well. The two main risks are unwanted pregnancy and STDs.

Facts About Pregnancy

Pregnancy can happen in ways that teens often may not realize. Here are some ways that pregnancy can happen.

Pregnancy can occur anytime during a female's menstrual cycle. Menstruation is the monthly discharge of blood, fluid, and tissue in nonpregnant females. Girls can get pregnant during their period.

Pregnancy can happen the first time a male and female have intercourse.

Pregnancy can happen if intercourse occurs while the couple is standing up.

Pregnancy can happen if sperm are near the vagina or enter it from the outside through underwear.

Douching right after sex does not prevent pregnancy. Douching is cleansing the inside of the vagina with a special solution.

Pregnancy can occur even if the male withdraws his penis before ejaculation, or the release of semen.

Counselors at these hotlines can provide information on pregnancy options.

Emergency Contraception Hotline
1-800-584-9911

Planned Parenthood Federation
1-800-230-PLAN

Abortion Hotline
1-800-772-9100

National Adoption Counseling Service
1-800-341-5959

If Pregnancy Happens

It can be scary to find out you are pregnant. If you or your partner becomes pregnant, it's important to talk with a trusted adult. That person can help you explore your options. You may be afraid to tell your parents. However, many parents will help their children deal with complicated issues like pregnancy. Other trusted adults can help you as well. You may know another relative or a teacher, counselor, or school nurse who can offer advice.

Options for an Unplanned Pregnancy

You may not have planned to get pregnant. If you do become pregnant, you will need a plan. You and your partner will need to make some hard choices. Your options include:

Keeping the baby and being a single parent

Keeping the baby and raising it with your boyfriend or girlfriend

Keeping the baby and getting married

Placing the baby for adoption

Having an abortion to end the pregnancy

Condoms, the "shot," and the Pill can all help prevent pregnancy. Condoms also can prevent the spread of some STDs. Abstinence prevents both pregnancy and STDs.

None of these choices is simple. Girls who are pregnant need to make a decision they can live with. Try not to rush your decision, but start to think about options right away.

Girls who choose to give birth to their baby need medical care as soon as possible. Staff at a clinic can make sure a girl and her fetus are healthy. Early checkups can improve a baby's chances for good health.

Adoption allows other people to become a child's legal parents. Adoptions can be done independently. That means the birth mother or birth parents can choose the adoptive parents. Adoptions also can be done through an agency. These adoptions may limit the birth mother's involvement. A birth mother must sign a Consent to Adoption form after the birth. Only at this point is the adoption final. Once the adoption is legal, the birth mother cannot change her mind.

Abortion ends a pregnancy early. Most clinics do abortions only during the first three months of a pregnancy. Abortions after that time are more risky and expensive.

The telephone book lists local organizations under *Pregnancy Counseling*. These organizations offer confidential advice. That means your conversation will not be shared with anyone else.

Neil's penis feels itchy and painful. He's had a burning feeling for several days. **Neil Is Stunned**
Neil is embarrassed, but he asks his mom to take him to the doctor.

The doctor asks Neil a bunch of questions. Then the doctor tests a small sample of discharge, or substance, released from Neil's penis. The test results come back quickly. Neil has a bacterial disease called gonorrhea. Neil cannot believe this. He wishes he had never had sex.

STDs Can Happen to Anyone

Many people, teens as well as adults, do not understand how sex spreads disease. You cannot look at someone and tell whether he or she has any STDs. Often people who have an STD do not realize it themselves. Some people never have symptoms, or evidence of the disease. With some STDs, symptoms can take months or years to appear.

STDs are spread through sexual contact with a person who is already infected. The mixing of body fluids during sexual activity can spread these diseases. Semen and vaginal secretions carry the germs that cause these diseases.

Some common types of STDs are genital warts, gonorrhea, herpes, HIV and AIDS, syphilis, and chlamydia. A virus causes genital warts, herpes, and HIV. These viral conditions can be treated, but they can never be cured. Bacteria cause gonorrhea, syphilis, and chlamydia. If found early, these bacterial diseases can be cured with antibiotics.

The only way to guarantee you won't get an STD is not to have sex. Condoms and dental dams can lower your chance of getting some STDs. However, even these barriers are not foolproof. Anyone who is sexually active should get a routine medical exam at least once a year. The chart on the next page lists some hotlines that can provide information about STDs.

Fast
Fact

Helpful Numbers for More Information About STDs

National AIDS Hotline
1-800-342-AIDS

National STD Hotline
1-800-227-8922

Safe Choice Hotline
1-800-878-2437

Points to Consider

Why do you think many teens have unprotected sex?

What kinds of things do you think teens need to know about the responsibilities of sex?

How many STDs do you know about? How could you learn more about STDs?

Chapter Overview

Breaking up can hurt.

Sometimes couples need to break up. They may not be a good match. They may make one another feel bad. They may be bored.

You can survive a breakup. You can use what you learn in one relationship to improve your next relationship.

Be gentle if you break up with someone. Chances are, others will hear how you handled the breakup. People who disregard their partner's feelings often end up being treated badly themselves.

Chapter 7

Breaking Up

Emma's boyfriend, Chris, just told her **Emma Feels Awful** he wants to break up. The two had been dating for more than a year. Emma cannot imagine life without Chris.

Chris told Emma, "I just want to be with my guy friends for a while. I'm too young to be in such a serious relationship. I hope we can still be friends, Em."

"Chris, I don't know if I want to be friends with you. I feel so hurt." Emma couldn't keep from crying.

Emma needs time to figure things out. She feels lost and alone. Tomorrow she will call her friend Miriam and talk. For now, she just wants to cry.

Myth: Breaking up is always hard.

Fact: Sometimes breaking up is not hard. Sometimes it is a relief for couples who have little in common.

Myth: There's something wrong with you if someone breaks up with you.

Fact: The breakup may have little to do with you. The other person may not be ready for the relationship. Breakups happen to everyone.

Breaking up can be difficult, but sometimes it can be a good thing to do. Breaking up can free you from someone who is not good for you. It can give you time with friends again. You can have time for your own hobbies and interests.

When Breaking Up Is Good to Do

Often breaking up does not feel good. It can hurt and make you feel sad. Those are normal feelings. Suddenly not being part of a couple can be hard. You may miss the person you used to date and the things you did together. Breaking up may be necessary under some circumstances.

The relationship is unequal.

People in a relationship need to feel like equals. That means both people feel they give and get from the other. A couple may be unequal if one person decides everything or pays for everything. The person with the power tries to control the relationship. That can make both people feel bad. The powerless person may resent the other person. The person who controls the relationship may feel burdened. That person may feel responsible for both people.

Your partner is putting on too much pressure.
It is hard to be happy when someone you care about is pressuring you. Often two people want very different things from a relationship. The differences in what a couple expects can create tension. If the two cannot agree, breaking up may be the best solution.

Your partner is hurting you physically or emotionally.
No one has the right to hurt anyone. It is never okay to hit, slap, or punch a partner. It is not okay to insult or slight a partner either. A couple needs to respect one another. You shouldn't stay with someone who makes you feel bad about yourself.

You are no longer interested in your partner.
Many relationships are not meant to last forever. Sometimes a couple grows bored with one another. Sometimes people develop new interests. They may miss doing the things they did before they became part of a couple. Sometimes one person starts liking someone new. Those are all signs that the relationship is coming to an end.

When Someone Breaks Up With You

Here are some tips on how to handle a breakup.

It's alright to be sad. It is normal to cry. Sometimes crying can help you feel better. It releases your emotions.

You may want to be alone for a while. Some people like to write down their feelings. You may want to spend time thinking about what happened. Just don't spend all your time alone. Don't think only of the breakup. Try to learn from it, and then move on.

Talk about the breakup. Get support from friends or trusted adults.

Get busy. Pick up an old hobby or learn a new skill. Take guitar lessons. Volunteer to help clean a park. Help an older neighbor. Get a part-time job.

Laugh. A funny movie may take your mind off your sadness. Even a book of jokes may lighten your mood. Laughing can help you feel better.

"Although breaking up is never fun, it's survivable. Remember that you're a whole person just as you are, and you don't need to be involved with someone else to be fun, likeable, or interesting."
—Chris
(author of "How to Cope with a Painful Breakup"an article from www.teenwire.com)

When You Do the Breaking Up

If you choose to break up with someone, think about how it would feel to be on the other end. It is a good idea to let your boyfriend or girlfriend down gently. It may allow you to be friends later on. It also may help your reputation.

Accept your feelings. It is okay for you to be sad, too. You may be relieved that you ended the relationship, but you may still feel sad. You do not need to feel guilty about making the decision to break up. You did what you thought was right for you.

"Love is like the measles; we all have to go through it."
—Jerome K. Jerome

Advice for the Couple

Don't badmouth your former boyfriend or girlfriend. What you say about the breakup could influence other people's opinions about you. Someone else may decide not to date you because of the mean words you said about your ex.

Look forward, not backward. You may feel as if you will never love again, but most likely you will. You can learn from your experience. You can think about what you liked and disliked about that relationship. What would you do differently next time? Your next relationship may be better because you learned from the last one.

Points to Consider

What would you say to break up kindly with someone?

How would you feel if someone broke up with you cruelly?

Why do you think most breakups happen?

How could you help a friend who is sad about a breakup? What three nice things could you say to that friend?

What kinds of things do not help someone who has just broken up?

Chapter Overview

Respect yourself and others will respect you, too.

There is no magic formula for dating success.

Talking is the best way to get to know a person.

Make time for yourself even while you date.

Love and sex are not the same.

You will recover from a breakup.

Chapter 8

Important Stuff to Remember

Dating can be fun, but it also can be scary. It is normal to have mixed feelings about dating, romance, love, and sex. You may want to keep these points in mind:

1. Respect yourself and others will respect you, too.
How you treat yourself often influences how others treat you. The more comfortable you are with yourself, the more success you will have with other people.

2. There is no magic formula for dating success.

It takes time to feel comfortable dating. The more you date, the more relaxed you may feel about it. Still, you do not need to rush into dating. Wait until you feel ready to have a boyfriend or girlfriend.

3. Talking is the best way to get to know a person.

You do not need fancy pickup lines to talk with someone you like. Just ask that special person what he or she likes. Get to know that person's friends and hobbies.

4. Make time for yourself even while you date.

Being part of a couple can feel great, but do not neglect your other interests. Continue to spend time with other friends, and save some time to be alone. Even the most loving and committed couples still need time apart.

5. Love and sex are not the same.

Love is the most powerful feeling in the world. You can love someone without touching him or her. Sex is an act that can feel good, but it also can complicate relationships. Sex can lead to pregnancy or disease. It is important to use protection against pregnancy and STDs.

6. You will recover from a breakup.

Couples break up for many reasons. It may feel like the end of the world, but you will recover. You can try to learn from the breakup. Sooner or later you will meet other people.

Points to Consider

How do you think self-respect affects how others treat you?

Why is it important to spend time by yourself when you are in a relationship?

What would you say if the person you were dating said, "If you really loved me, you would have sex with me?"

What is the best way to meet and get to know a new person?

Glossary

abstinence (AB-stuh-nenss)—a choice not to have sexual intercourse

date rape (DAYT RAYP)—sexual assault involving two people who know each other and may have a relationship together

dating (DAYT-ing)—when two people interested in each other romantically go out together

emotion (i-MOH-shun)—a feeling such as sadness, fear, happiness, or joy

genitals (JEN-eh-tuhlz)—sex organs; male genitals are the penis and testicles; female genitals include the vagina and clitoris.

heterosexual (HET-tur-oh-SEK-shoo-wuhl)—relating to attraction to members of the opposite sex; straight.

homosexual (HO-moh-SEK-shoo-wuhl)—relating to attraction to members of the same sex; males who have homosexual attractions are called gay; females who have homosexual attractions are called lesbian.

hormone (HOR-mohn)—a chemical in the human body that determines how people grow and develop sexually; a chemical that controls body functions.

infatuation (in-FACH-yoo-ay-shun)—a feeling of being wildly attracted to or in love with someone; also known as having a crush on someone.

intimacy (IN-tuh-muh-see)—a feeling of being very closely connected to another person

love (LUHV)—a strong feeling of caring about another person

masturbation (mass-ter-BAY-shun)—pleasurable touching or rubbing of the genitals in a sexual way

pregnant (PREG-nuhnt)—when a female has an embryo or fetus growing inside her body

relationship (ri-LAY-shuhn-ship)—the way in which people get along together

sex (SEKS)—the two genders, male and female; the act of sexual intercourse.

sexually transmitted disease (SEK-shoo-wuhl-lee transs-MIT-ted duh-ZEEZ)—a disease spread from person to person through sexual contact; also called STD.

For More Information

Basso, Michael J. *The Underground Guide to Teenage Sexuality: An Essential Handbook for Today's Teens and Parents.* Minneapolis: Fairview Press, 1997.

Bell, Ruth. *Changing Bodies, Changing Lives: A Book for Teens on Sex and Relationships.* New York: Times Books, 1998.

Endersbe, Julie K. *Healthy Sexuality: What Is It?* Mankato, MN: Capstone Press, 2000.

Moe, Barbara. *Everything You Need to Know About Sexual Abstinence.* New York: Rosen, 1995.

Stoppard, Miriam, and Sally Artz. *Sex Ed: Growing Up, Relationships, and Sex.* New York: DK Publishing, 1997.

Useful Addresses and Internet Sites

Coalition for Positive Sexuality
3712 North Broadway
Suite 191
Chicago, IL 60613
http://www.positive.org

The National Coalition for Gay, Lesbian,
Bisexual and Transgender Youth (!OUTPROUD!)
369 Third Street
Suite B362
San Rafael, CA 94901
http://www.outproud.org

Ottawa Rape Crisis Centre
PO Box 20206
Ottawa, ON K1N 9P4
CANADA
http://www.intranet.ca/~orcc

Planned Parenthood
810 Seventh Avenue
New York, NY 10019
1-800-230-PLAN
http://www.teenwire.com

Go Ask Alice
http://www.goaskalice.columbia.edu
Answers teens' questions about relationships,
sexuality, and health

Interrace Haven
http://www.austin.quik.com/~crusader/
irhaven.html
Focuses on mixed-race relationships and issues
from dating to marriage and adoption

SEX, ETC.
http://www.sxetc.org
Web site for teens by teens that discusses
relationships, sexuality, and other topics

TeenCentral.Net
http://www.teencentral.net
Includes library of teen stories about
relationships

Index

abortion, 44

abstinence, 36, 44, 46, 58

adoption, 44

alcohol, 30

appearance, 14–15

attractions, 15
   being comfortable with, 8, 21

birth control, 34. *See also* condoms

breaking up, 26, 36, 49–54, 59

changing behavior, 28–29, 34

CityKids, 21

communication, 16, 33

compromise, 26

condoms, 35, 44, 46

counselors, 43, 44

crushes, 16, 17, 19–23
   same-sex, 8–9

date rape, 30

dating
   why people do it, 6–7

dental dams, 35, 46

double-dating, 13, 30

drugs, 30

emotional intimacy, 26

estrogen, 7

eye contact, 16

family. *See* parents

feeling
   embarrassed, 13, 17, 30
   jealous, 27, 36
   sad, 50, 52, 53
   shy, 13, 16, 17
   upset, 29, 49

fighting, 27

flirting, 13

friends, 7, 19, 26, 27, 29, 33, 41, 52
   making new, 14–16
   making time for, 31, 49, 58

gonorrhea, 45, 46

grooming habits, 14

group dating, 30

happiness, 10, 25

HIV/AIDS, 46, 47

homosexual, 8–9

hormones, 7

hotline, 43, 46–47

impressions, first, 14–15

infatuation. *See* crushes

love, 19, 20–22, 27, 28, 54, 58
   self, 10

Index continued